George Rich
Struggling With My Soul

Library and Archives Canada Cataloguing in Publication

Rich, George, 1962-, author
        Struggling with my soul / George Rich.

Originally published: St. John's, Nfld. : Harrish Press, 2000.
ISBN 978-0-9939095-3-5 (softcover)

        1. Rich, George, 1962-. 2. Naskapi Indians--Biography.
3. Readers for new literates. I. Mamu Tshishkutamashutau-Innu
Education Inc, issuing body II. Title.
PE1126.N43R53 2017   428.6'2   C2017-902570-8

© 2017 **Mamu Tshishkutamashutau Innu Education**
Copyright for the text is retained by the author.
All rights reserved. This book or any portion thereof may only be reproduced for educational purposes. Any other reproduction whatsoever cannot occur without the express written permission of the author and publisher, except for the use of brief quotations.

MTIE gratefully acknowledges the funding support for this publication from the New Paths Program, Indigenous and Northern Affairs Canada, Government of Canada.

Boulder Publications acknowledges financial support from the Government of Newfoundland and Labrador through the Publisher's Assistance Program.

Editor: Camille Fouillard
Cover and inside design: Vessela Brakalova, Vis-à-Vis Graphics Inc.

Published by: Boulder Publications Ltd.
http://www.boulderpublications.ca

Mamu Tshishkutamashutau Innu Education
http://www.innueducation.ca

CONTENTS

FOREWORD	1
THE PROMISED LAND	7
COMING OF AGE IN NATUASHISH	15
A BOY BETWEEN WORLDS	23
ELDERS, LEADERS, COWBOYS AND INDIANS	33
COMING APART	37
HEALING	45
WAKING THE TRUE INNU SPIRIT	53
CROSSING THE WHITE LINE	57
WHERE I BELONG	63
THE ROCKY ROAD TO SELF-DETERMINATION	69
ACKNOWLEDGEMENTS	89

A ceremonial caribou robe, belonging to George's paternal grandfather Meshkeia (Sam Rich). The designs were painted by his grandmother Kaukatshish (Manakanet). The designs have special meaning; they come through dreams, instructions from the guardian spirits.

FOREWORD

This is one of a series of four books, developed for **Exploring Memory, Finding Meaning**, a special project of the Adult Basic Education Writing Network. The books all began in a workshop where writers shared ideas and life stories, as well as thoughts about the fears and joys of writing itself. During the workshop, writers used photographs of people and places as doorways to the past, as ways to get at their memories and the stories that are important to them. Writers wrote about whatever the photographs brought to mind, then read their drafts aloud. Other writers and workshop leaders gave comments and asked questions. Then the writers went home to face the winter and the work of rewriting alone. Like most writing, this book is a product of both community and solitary work.

George Rich's **Struggling With My Soul** is a story of growing up caught between two worlds. The author is a Labrador Innu whose family and people gave up their nomadic way of life to settle in Davis Inlet. But the promises of a better life in the new place quickly turned to alcoholism, despair and tragedy. Rich's story is one of a people coming apart, but it is also a story of healing—and of the hard work it takes to put one's life, one's soul and one's community back together. Readers who are not familiar with the Innu language will come across new words here. There is **Natuashish**—the wonderful winter encampment where the caribou come. There is **Kuekuatsheu**, who in Innu legend creates the earth with the help of animals. Readers should not worry about how to pronounce the words, but enjoy the stories behind them instead. The language of any culture is an entrance to a new world. Readers who speak one language may want to think about what it would be like to always live between two languages, two cultures.

George's book was originally published in 2000. This new edition includes an epilogue, in which George writes about the relocation of the Davis Inlet Mushuau Innu to Natuashish, as well as some of his thoughts about child welfare, education and as well as the involvement of the Labrador Innu in resource developments and the land claims process.

Davis Inlet, or Utshimassits—Place of the Boss, 1970

THE PROMISED LAND

The northerly wind calmed as we landed on the beach of the new Davis Inlet. Waves splashed against our 15-foot punt, in which 10 people were crammed together.

We had often traveled to this place before. It was across from the old Davis Inlet. The site had been chosen by the missionary and his newly appointed chief, a respected elder. Now this place had become the promised land. There was talk of a huge store, a church and a big school that would take all the children age five and up.

My parents were not church-going people. They were not easily tamed by the missionary. But they decided to set up their tent near the church and school that were being built. Almost all the men in the community were being trained and employed as carpenters to build the new community. People set up their tents near

the stream that would be used for drinking and cooking. My parents immediately set their nets into the water to catch the Arctic char that swarmed the area.

"We've got to eat," my father said. "I don't think we will receive a pay cheque. We've got to work first."

"Why do we have to camp here near everybody?" my mother asked him. "There is no privacy here. It seems that all the other tents are camped so close together and there will be a lot of noise from the teenagers who always prowl in the nights."

"Your brother Kaniuekutat and my brother David will also camp near here," my father told her. "Besides that, we can try to go to church more often and maybe the priest will start noticing us. We never did get much clothing that he gave away." He went on. "And we'll able to get a house right away instead of waiting forever. They promised that they'd build 10 houses this summer and we might get lucky."

This kind of talk went on for days. As people arrived and set up their tents near the beaches, they talked about what kind of houses they wanted. They wanted running water and full basements. They thought that now all the things said at the priest's house would finally come true. The talk of houses brought excitement and joy to the women in the tent city of the new Davis Inlet.

No one knew what would happen in the next decades on that tiny island off the mainland of Labrador.

Before we settled in Davis Inlet, my people, the Innu, had always led a nomadic life. We did not stay in one place. The Innu traveled to and from Quebec's northern shores, migrated with the caribou, and had regular contact with relatives in Schefferville and Fort Chimo.

> We hauled water from a nearby stream that didn't freeze in the winter.

Our land was known as Nitassinan. In its interior was a traditional gathering place where festivities and marriages took place. This place was known as Tshinuatipish. It was also known as "Indian House Lake." Innu had met in this place long before trading posts were established in the late 1800s. We continued to meet there until a lot of Innu people were forced to settle in one place.

In the new community of Davis Inlet, the houses were in a line from east to west. My family lived in the east end away from the school and the church and store. My parents were among the last people to get the houses that were built. They were away in the bay in the fall when the houses were given away by the new council.

I remember when we first moved to our new house. It wasn't equipped with water or sewer. We hauled water from a nearby stream that didn't freeze in the winter. We were at least one kilometre from the school and store. The store manager ran the post office too. There were many things to order from Eaton's catalogue—record players, clothes, radios. Walking from one end of the community to the other, from my house to the store, I would hear Hank Williams wailing from our neighbour's house. As I reached another dwelling, I would listen to Johnny Cash. At the far end of the village were the teenagers, who had gone away to school and come back for the summer. Their music rocked the air with Elvis Presley and CCR.

It was a beautiful setting. There were three hills to explore, a wooded area, and at the east end of the community, a stream where we children soaked and swam in the warm, muddy waters.

Davis Inlet lies under one of the hills, and as children we often went there to see if a coastal boat was on the horizon. The site was chosen for a coastal boat to get closer to the wharf and I suppose for the new airstrip that was built 15 years later but was already being planned. In the old Davis Inlet, coastal boats used to anchor far away from the shallow harbour, and its huge hills and steep, rocky land made it hard to build an airstrip or houses.

◆◆◆◆◆◆◆◆◆◆◆◆◆◆◆◆◆◆◆◆◆◆◆◆◆◆◆◆◆◆◆

A large rock in the centre of the new community was a great hangout in the evening. This is also where the nuns and teachers lived in the two-story dwelling with running water. We kept the nuns and teachers awake at night and played pranks on the poor nuns. We would knock at their door and they would sometimes chase us. This was our main entertainment. They never caught us because we hid under the steps below their entrance way. Sometimes someone would run out of luck. Then they would tell on us. The nuns would give us an earful in the school lobby, and the pranks would stop for a little while.

There was an old bell that the nuns rang every morning to summon us to school. One time my friend tied a rope to its centre using black thread. He hid a few metres away and rang the bell by pulling the ropes. A nun would come running to see who was abusing the bell but she couldn't see anybody. My friend would stop ringing the bell as she came closer. This went on until she saw the thread. The following morning there was another earful, with reminders that the bell could only be rung when school was in session or for emergencies.

We had our fun. Near the rock in the centre of the village, usually on Thursdays and Sundays, there would be soccer games and our own version of baseball. We only

My Mom and me

used two bases. The idea was that you had to hit the ball three times, and if you did, you had to run to the other base before somebody hit you with a ball. If the ball hit you, you were out. If a teammate got stuck at first base, it was your job to get them back to the home base without getting hit by the ball. If the other team managed to catch your ball while in the air, your team was out. There were usually two teams but no score was kept; it was just for fun.

As we grew up, we often got our water from the brook because the community pump was usually broke. The endless need to haul water was quite a workload for any teenager. Children hauled wood too. I remember at about age 12 going with my brother to haul wood on the komatik, sometimes using a dog team.

With the two of us, getting wood was always an adventure. My brother was two years older than I was, and much stronger and wiser. After hours of cutting and loading wood, I would often make him angry for I was clumsy and slow. But this was also to his advantage. He played some memorable tricks on me.

One time we hauled wood my father had cut about a kilometre away. We used the dog team, and when we finished putting everything on the komatik, my brother said I was the faster runner and I should guide the dogs along the trail to Davis Inlet. After running for a few minutes, I stopped to catch my breath.

He kept flattering me that I was faster and could run without rest. As I was leading the dogs, I looked around to see if he was pushing the load from behind. I caught a glimpse of him lying down and enjoying the ride while I was suffering from exhaustion.

Once we cut wood in an uphill area. The trail was narrow and it would be tricky to get back down. I am sure he knew that as well. If we hit one of the trees when we went downhill, we might break the komatik bars and we would be stuck there for the rest of the day. And we would have to face our father with the news. My brother stayed ahead of me and out of trouble as I guided the komatik downhill. I managed to swing it the wrong way and it hit a tree. My brother cursed the daylights out of me and we had to rearrange the load just to get the komatik on solid ground. My brother said he would tell on me and we started fighting and arguing. In the end I got thrown in a snow bank. Then I ran away. I told him I was not going to help him. He had to do all the work.

He cursed and shouted death threats. I got away and watched him from a distance. He changed his tone a little bit and promised he would lead the dogs from now on. I could sit on the komatik for a change—if I helped him put all the wood on the komatik. I did and then he told me that I had hurt his knee when I led the komatik into the tree. He blackmailed me with telling our father what I did. I thought it would be in my best interest to lead the dogs again. Of course, he sat on the komatik the rest of the way. Miraculously, his knee was healed before we reached home.

COMING OF AGE IN NATUASHISH

My father managed to save enough money to purchase the snowmobile we needed, for he had worked in a fish camp most of his life. He was a fish guide for the outfitters for a number of years. He and a friend went out to work summers in a fish camp in a place known as Hunt River. We would not see him until the end of August when he came home for the season. He was usually gone for a couple of months. Then he would come back with enough money to purchase an outboard motor and canoe and snowmobile to use on the fall trip to Natuashish, where he would set up a winter camp. There, he would set a net for Arctic char on their way to the lake. He would tell us that someday the caribou would go by the pond.

After we did our chores, we skated and fished. When the pond was frozen for a few days, we would ice-fish for trout along the shore. When the ice was safe, the skates we got from the priest came in handy. Once the Natuashish froze solid, we would skate around it, the strong wind pushing us a little faster to the other side of the pond.

But the most memorable experience I had growing up in Natuashish was when my father's prediction came true. I might have been 13 years or older back then. That was my first chance to shoot a caribou, after years of trying and not succeeding. The elders said it was the first time in 30 years the caribou herd had come across little Natuashish Pond. It was exciting for any hunter to see such a great herd.

They came around the point in great numbers, and a week passed when we saw the magnificent herd pass by our camp.

The spirits of the hunters went up like rockets blasted into outer space. There were screams of joy and tears from our mothers. Hunters grabbed their rifles to hop on the skidoos to get their first kill. The longing for fresh meat was strong after a diet of fish and small game. The hunters quickly went to the wooded area on the other side of the lake, planning to meet the caribou when they came in close. The recently frozen Natuashish was quickly forgotten as men hurried across.

My mother told me to keep quiet and listen for gunshots. We could hear gunshots but we couldn't see the hunters. We could see the caribou going in the direction where the hunters were hiding and taking their shots. Only an hour had passed when we sighted the first skidoo returning with fresh kill.

The women of the camp searched for butcher knives to skin the caribou, shouting in frustrated tones about where they had left their knives and files. Of course, I had used the file earlier to sharpen my skates. I'd forgot where I'd put it last. One of my siblings told my mother that I was the last one who had used the file. Only after she turned everything upside down did the file and the knife turn up. The kill was skinned and the cooking pots and teapots were made ready.

It was in the late evening when my father and the others showed up. They slit the throats of the caribou they'd killed so the meat would not spoil overnight. They talked on into the night, and I listened to the conversations of my father and uncle about the kill and what they needed for the winter. The next morning the real work began. The hunters quickly built a cache to store the frozen meat for the winter and hauled the carcasses in.

The news of the caribou spread quickly around Davis Inlet. The hunters of Davis Inlet arrived the following morning across the recently frozen water. The visitors would kill what they needed. My older brother and another man got their caribou. I had yet to get my own caribou. I helped my mother butcher the caribou and store

Hettasch collection

Hunters

it in the rafters, while my brother and father hauled the meat. I was left behind as usual to do the chores of getting the water and cutting the wood.

My uncle had left his rifle behind just in case the caribou came near our camp. My mother said to be careful if I had to use the gun because I had never fired a high-powered rifle before. It was late in the day when I saw my opportunity to shoot my first caribou. The others saw two caribou come directly towards our camp. My mother and aunt told me to wait until they were closer, and I had to walk a few hundred metres away from camp to get my shot. As the two wandering caribou came closer to where I hid, my hands were trembling and I started to sweat. I aimed to shoot and squeezed the trigger but nothing happened. Now they were only a few feet away. I squeezed again—nothing!

When the caribou spotted me, they ran towards me. They were fairly close, and I couldn't even shoot. They ran towards the woods and I was left there, stunned. I didn't even know that there was a safety lock on the rifle. I didn't know how to use the gun. I felt ashamed and humiliated. I gave up, but I didn't go home to the camp, feeling that my siblings would mock me, especially my older brother when he got home. Finally, tired and hungry, I went home and told my mother what had happened. I said the gun was jammed and I couldn't shoot it. My brother-in-law and my brother came back from the hunt then, and my younger sibling told them about the incident. They checked the gun and saw that the safety lock was on. They took it off, aimed the gun at a target and fired. My brother laughed his head off. My in-law told me jokingly that I shouldn't get married. If I did, I would probably starve my wife and children, because I couldn't even shoot a gun. The mocking at my expense carried on for days in our tent.

It was a few weeks later before I got another chance. My brother and I were hauling out the carcasses when he spotted caribou. They were still plentiful in our area. He had shown me how to use the gun before we set out. He told me not to be nervous and to be very careful where I pointed the gun. If I didn't do what he instructed me to do, he would punch the daylights out of me. I got ready and took a firing position. Still inexperienced in handling a gun, I missed many times. I think I closed my eyes during the first shots, as I was afraid of the gun, and it hurt my shoulder as I fired. I finally had a lucky shot and one of the bulls fell hard to the snow.

My first reaction was: if only my mother or father could see me now. Although my parents were impressed that I shot my first caribou and praised me, I must have felt at least 10 feet taller than my brother at the time. I had finally become a man, my father told me. And since we had enough meat to last the winter, I was told to clean and butcher the big bull with the help of my mother. My brother-in-law told me that I might have a chance yet not to starve my wife and children. And so I got my first caribou in November.

Young Innu men in Utshimassits, 1970s

A BOY BETWEEN WORLDS

In places like Natuashish, the Innu world went on as before. But in the new settlement of Davis Inlet, the children would be educated in English, a language foreign to them. The Innu would struggle to keep their own values and beliefs and way of life. Already the missionaries had mocked our spiritual beliefs. Our fundamental rights as people had been violated—how and where we lived and how we governed ourselves had been taken over by another culture. The promised land became a shambles of despair and poverty.

> I sometimes wonder what would happen now if Innu people entered a foreign land and tried to make the rules and regulations, and tried to impose their cultural and spiritual beliefs on other people. What would happen if the Innu tried to force others to speak their language? People of European descent need to take the time to think of how hurtful and degrading that can be. Maybe then they will understand why there is so much anger and suicide among Labrador's Aboriginal peoples.

As a young boy, I watched, fascinated, as the world of my people changed. Snowmobiles quickly replaced dog teams; outboard motors replaced canoes and paddles. All the new conveniences cost money. But work was scarce and there were few ways to get money. People also needed to learn how to manage the money they earned. All of a sudden, money was important in Innu culture in ways it never was before.

~Siblings Katie, Mathias, Eric and Toon, and mother Matnin

When food was scarce in Davis Inlet, my parents walked all the way to the hunting grounds. Even though they now lived in houses, families still prepared for their fall hunt when they would camp near the mainland and near the rivers. There, they caught the winter supply of Arctic char, small game like porcupine and small birds. They would leave the community that had been built for them behind.

In the late 1960s my parents and five other families traveled to hunting grounds where caribou usually were plentiful. This may be the last time I know of that people traveled quite a distance by dog team to hunt caribou. The area was known as Border Beacon because of the new weather station there. The caretakers of the weather station would always share when the Innu ran out of grub like tea or sugar. It was fiercely cold on those barrens. I remember now how the five of us children were tucked in and bundled up in canvas. I am lucky to have this memory.

I also remember the day my younger brother was born in the country. I don't know how my mother survived the ordeal of harsh cold and all the pulling and shoving of the komatik. My father was pulling the sled with the help of three cranky dogs. There were blizzard conditions that day, and on the barrens wood was scarce. It must have been hard for my mother to keep warm through her labour.

Myself on the right in juniour high

We were sent to my uncle's tent to wait for the baby's arrival. We didn't know what was happening. All my father told us was that our mother was sick and we had to behave ourselves. This brought back fear and bad memories of the time she had to go away to hospital in North West River with TB. What was going on in our minds brought our usually energetic spirits to a halt for the day. My uncle told us not to worry because she was in good hands. Three midwives were taking care of her.

Late in the afternoon we had a little brother. As any child would do, we asked our father how the baby had arrived in our tent. He told us the baby was found crawling up to our tent that afternoon. Being curious, we set out to look for tracks and couldn't find any.

Because of the birth, my parents were forced to stay behind while other Innu families headed home. We had to wait until my mother started to gain her strength back. On the way home, I had to walk beside the komatik. I started to dislike my little brother. I told my mother quietly that she should have left him there where they had found him. He was taking my space where I would have enjoyed being bundled up against the cold.

~Mission, school and clinic building in Utshimassits, 1970

As we settled into the new community, we had to get used to new neighbours. There were teachers, nurses, store managers, and other new people to work with the Innu. These people were all white. The only jobs available to Innu were as janitors in the school and as relief workers for the hydro generating plant. The lucky ones who had been obedient to the missionary got the first chance at these jobs.

Many other people suddenly became dependent on welfare and family allowance cheques. Parents were told that in order to receive family allowances, they would have to send their children to school. The Innu were not supposed to take their children out of school to go in the country, although this was an important part of our way of life. Few people struggled against the new rule. One missionary tried to find a way around it. He encouraged the families to camp about a mile outside the community.

The missionary and the new leaders that had been parachuted in to look after us had begun to realize something. The restless Innu could not easily turn away from their way of life and move to a more permanent settlement. Almost immediately, they began to turn to alcohol.

The new school opened in the late fall. There were nuns and brothers to supposedly educate us children. From the beginning, the new language and the outside world sidetracked our way of thinking. We had to learn quickly about the Prime Ministers of Canada. We had to be patriotic like any Canadian child and learn to sing *O Canada*.

But we had our own culture. I remember hearing as a child the legends about the *Tshakapesh*. He is a folk hero who destroys *Atshen*, a mystical cannibal who hunted down the Innu. Eventually, Tshakapesh and his sister went to live on the moon. Now when we heard about men landing on the moon we were confused. When the teacher asked one of the Innu students who was the first man on the moon, the Innu child replied *"Tshakapesh."*

In religion class, our beliefs clashed again. I remember a priest asking a student who created the earth. The student answered without hesitation, *"Kuekuatsheu."* There are comical legends about Kuekuatsheu, a man who deceives everyone who comes across his path. He is also known as creator of the earth with the help of the animals. This was another of our beloved legends that soon went down the tubes.

Of all the things we were taught during our first year of school, religion was the greatest torment. The missionary had graphic pictures of the devil and demons that looked so horrible, they stayed in my mind late at night. His thundering voice preaching about hell and fire left us with the impression that he was the saviour of our people.

Despite the demons, I always enjoyed school, and I was eager to learn about other things and other places around the world. I stayed in that school until grade eight. We had to do grade nine outside of the community. It would be my first time ever on the island of Newfoundland. At first it was culture shock. I didn't understand what was going on in my new surroundings. The first day of class I was surprised to come face to face with Brothers again. I was frightened and concerned about

what they would do to us. It took a while to adjust. The new teachers weren't so bad, but I could not really trust them. In the late 1960s, I had been sexually assaulted by Brothers in Davis Inlet.

I never did finish the second semester. I had trouble keeping up with other students in the class. During one of our English classes, the teacher told us to write an essay on Pontiac, the car. I had no idea what a Pontiac was. If he had suggested writing about the snowmobile, I would probably have gotten a good mark on the essay. I didn't do a lot of the assignments because I didn't understand them.

At the age of fifteen, I'd had it with school. My friends and I went back to Davis Inlet. For a few years, I just hung out. There weren't many opportunities for work or training.

Our summer youth employment in Davis Inlet was make-work projects, hauling the store goods from the coastal boats to the warehouse. Almost every summer, I worked in community cleanup. The sale of a catch of Arctic char to the nuns brought enough money for a round trip to Nain on a coastal boat. Either of the two coastal boats was a chance to get out of the community for a night, a quick getaway. A lot of times we would go without paying the fare and we would share with others who paid for a room. We used their tickets that were already punched by the purser. Sometimes they didn't even bother to look for stowaways. No wonder Marine Atlantic is in trouble now.

Our one-night vacations in Nain, the most northerly community in Labrador, put some variety in my boring teenage life. We eagerly awaited the first boat of the year, which usually got in around mid-July.

A boat expected was always excitement. When we knew a boat was coming that day, we would climb the hill at the back of the community and use it as a crow's nest. If we saw the boat on the horizon, looking south heading towards Davis Inlet, we would yell down below that the boat was coming. Those who heard us sometimes climbed the steep hill just to see what all the fuss was about. Adults would climb

~My father Napaien rowing

up with their binoculars and stay for hours, looking for wildlife or just passing the time away. The hill was a good place to play cowboys and Indians or war games or to escape from the mosquitoes.

With the first boat of summer, new store goods would arrive, including cans of pop and chips that would be a treat for the next few months. When nobody was around, those of us who unloaded it would reward ourselves with a soft drink and bags of chips after a hard day's work. Sometimes the coastal boats anchored out in the harbor, and collector boats brought the goods to be unloaded at a small wharf. The store manager and stock handlers of the government store marked down everybody who worked, and how many hours we worked. The next morning we had to wait in line to collect our wages. Sometimes our wages disappeared again before we left the store.

In the summer, the store had a new stock of fishing supplies—rods, reels and spinners. We fished daily, and it was the one thing I loved to do.

One time I tried to enlist in the army when a recruiter came by. I was told to travel to St. John's and meet certain people. I made my way up to Goose Bay and stayed in a hotel for the night. It was there I met with my half brother and his friend from Davis Inlet. They were working in Sheshatshiu at the lumberyard and were traveling back to Davis Inlet on a coastal boat the following morning.

After a few beers, they asked what I was doing in Goose Bay. At first I didn't want to say anything, but after a few beers, I told them about my plans. They laughed. They asked me how I could be in the army when I couldn't even shoot a caribou. How could I defend myself in a war when I didn't know how to use a gun? After a lot of beer, my wish to be in the army had flown away. After chatting with these supposedly wiser role models of mine, I decided to go back with them the next morning on the coastal boat. It was not long before I was caught up in my community's struggle to survive.

Kaniuekutat at gathering in Natuashish, 1992

ELDERS, LEADERS, COWBOYS AND INDIANS

When the life you lead is not an easy or very pleasant road to travel, you need a lot of support along the way. If you do a lot of crazy stuff when you are drinking, this will be one of the hurdles you have to jump in order to succeed. My uncle Kaniuekutat (John Poker) used to say this to me. He was my uncle on my mother's side and a respected elder in the community. I would visit him in the two-bedroom bungalow he shared with his daughter Katnen (Catherine) and her four children. Kaniuekutat used to drink when he was young but had been a sober man for many years. He sobered up on his own without the help of outside treatment centres because he wanted to quit and alcohol was getting him nowhere. He felt that stopping drinking was the only way to survive.

Kaniuekutat and other elders often advised us young leaders. At times we thought we were problem solvers for the great social illness that existed in our community. We often bragged about our understanding of the English language and the rules of governments. We assumed that the elders were not worth listening to. When elders wanted to run for band council elections, we young leaders mocked their old ways of thinking. We said what they knew was not relevant to this new world. We said their world was dead, and we had to have people who understood European culture and who could read and write. Band council elections gradually turned into a race that divided the elders and young leaders. How wrong we were! If we had included our elders in all of our meetings, things would have been different. We would have stayed in touch with our own culture.

Meeting the float plane, 1970s

I remember the first community elections held in the late 1970s, the first time leaders were not chosen by Innu traditions. It was the missionary who got the elections going. He followed the Municipalities Act, a provincial Act followed by all town councils in Newfoundland and Labrador. The Act itself is a thick book with everything in it from how to run your own government to dog control policy. This policy might have had something to do with the disappearance of the dog team in our lives. The snowmobile had replaced dog teams in our culture, something we had borrowed from our neighbours, the Inuit.

The Municipalities Act brought another new thing—taxes. My parents had to pay $10 a year. As such things came into the community, people tried to adapt. But there was no plan to provide jobs so that people could earn the money they now needed.

The people in power, outsiders who worked in the community, may have had good intentions. But there was little municipal funding. Most of the work was make-work projects like putting in a community pump where people could get their water, digging ditches, raking and hauling garbage to the dumps. Some funding was used to renovate the church, which was also used as a community hall.

We went there to see movies, such as westerns, everybody's favourite. The cowboys always won the war, so we couldn't help cheering for them instead of the Indians. Most people my age always wanted to be cowboys. I sometimes wonder if that was another part of the master plan to brainwash the Innu into thinking that White culture is superior to ours.

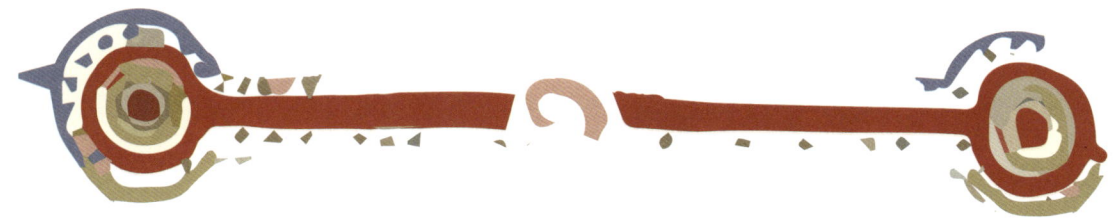

COMING APART

The new way of choosing leaders went against the old traditional ways by which the Innu ran their affairs. The Innu had always relied on the elders in the camp, and they had their way of selecting camp leaders, or *utshimauts*. There were many kinds of *utshimauts*. There was a camp *utshimau* and *utshimauts* for hunting. Almost everyone in the camp had a role to play.

The election system created division and took away the elders' traditional role. This new kind of leader was not like the traditional *utshimau*. Elections brought all the kinds of corruption elections can have. In our small community, people with large families could control band council elections and government. Also, anyone who had a lot of alcohol could win a seat on council. Now every year we have elections in Davis Inlet, mainly because people crave influence or business contracts or good employment from the council.

> People think of community government in terms of what power or favours they can get. What began as petty politics grew from a spark into a blazing fire that divides our community still today. The only way to extinguish the flames is to create a new way of electing community representatives. We need a way for everyone to have his or her say.

I loved the elections for all the booze brought in by the people who wanted the chief's job or councilor's position. When it was my turn to run, I used every trick

~Chief Joe Rich, Shushepiss 1971

I'd learned to get elected as band councilor. I had many tactics. Once I went out for the Liberal leadership convention when Len Sterling was elected leader. I quickly imitated the use of campaign buttons in the next band council election. I ordered the buttons and distributed them to my supporters. I once wore the campaign buttons as earrings when I was drunk and crazy at a party. I did it to get votes and laughs, but you can imagine how I felt the following morning.

The thrills and excitement lasted until I turned sober at the age of 29. After 17 years, I reached a point where I felt guilt and shame that I was serving only my own self-interest. I could see my own people struggling to survive on $500 a month on welfare for a family of five. Yet some elected leaders wouldn't even attend meetings unless they received an honorarium of $500 a day. It began to keep me awake at night. When we attended outside meetings, we received a per diem of $60 a day for expenses. We would stay for a number of days to get the full amount.

Perhaps I should have listened to my father. When I decided to run for election, I turned to him for support and advice. My father said I should go hunting caribou instead. I should have realized by now that my father never bought into all the changes happening around us. His beliefs and principles as an Innu gatherer and hunter were all he knew.

When the thrill went out of politics for me, I also realized we weren't achieving much of value. We were not doing enough for people who needed new homes. Alcoholism had rapidly increased. The band councils couldn't do a thing with their budgets and the governments of the day turned deaf ears to us. They ignored our pleas for the funding and resources we needed. We tried so hard to answer the needs of the people, but what could we do if nobody was listening?

Over the years I would chat with the elder on the Council about the way things were going. Once I asked if he was going to run in the next election. He just laughed lightly and told me that if I wanted to create any image for myself, I should know by now it was all an illusion. He said he ran in the elections for fun, something to do. He knew nothing was going to change. He told me that if things were going to change now, then it was in the works already, and it would happen so fast that we young leaders wouldn't be able to handle it. Looking back now, I realize he was right. When the federal government announced the relocation of Davis Inlet, all the things he told me were right there in front of our noses. We could not handle it.

The public meeting was held in the basement of the community bathhouse. The big question was: in what direction are we heading? We had a public forum about where we could get water and sewer, the topic on everybody's mind. The Band Council had hired an engineer to do studies on where we could get water, but still we had no answers. The drilling lasted for three years and the engineers drilled everywhere. The cost of the studies was sky-high. We were running out of ideas. The community joke was that we had so many drill holes in Davis Inlet, the whole island would soon sink.

It was then that the elders spoke about resettlement from the mainland 25 years ago, how water and sewer had been promised then, but never delivered. The elders urged

the young leaders to talk to the federal and provincial governments about the current conditions of the houses and the skin diseases of the Innu in Davis Inlet.

It was time to listen to the elders. We organized a meeting for federal and provincial representatives to come see first-hand how our people lived. We organized the public meeting in a tent setting, and we invited the media. The elders were very outspoken; they were not satisfied to get their water and dump their honey buckets outside in the freezing winter. We asked the bored bureaucrats what other Canadians lived in such conditions? Is it a Canadian standard to live like this? The questions from the elders were very powerful and touching. The federal and provincial officials told the Innu they would listen to their concerns and take them to their bosses in Ottawa. But the ongoing meetings were postponed and we never did receive the answer we wanted to hear.

> With encouragement from the elders, the leaders didn't give up. Somehow in the next few years, things seemed to fall into place. But first there had to be tragedy. The accidental burning of six children and the suicide attempts of teens created an uproar throughout Canada. People wanted to know what was going on in Davis Inlet and who was responsible for this mess. It wasn't a difficult decision to make when our crisis worker called to say that our teenagers were shouting and damaging the crisis centre. Apparently our tribal police spotted them just in time before they hurt themselves.

On the spot we made a decision to release the video to outside news agencies. We had to get the children out too. When we requested back-up from the RCMP, they turned us down, so with the help of the Innu Nation president, we chartered an aircraft in the early morning. It was then that the images of Davis Inlet scattered around the country.

We got few hours of sleep before hearing that the children we escorted out in the early morning were in a safe place. Now the real work had begun. All the media attention turned toward the social illness that had existed in our community for so long. A few months later the announcement was made: the Innu would move to the mainland site of our choice.

Good things were happening but we were left with the fact that six children had died in a house fire. My sister's grandchildren were burned. I believe the federal government decided to do something about Davis Inlet then, after it felt the heat from the Canadian public. It was certainly a turning point and eye opener for us to start to think about our children.

We asked the federal government to do an inquiry into why this pain and suffering was happening to Innu people. It turned us down. In the end, the Innu Nation and Band Council found the funds to do such a study. All the frustrations and grievances were told in Gathering Voices.

The reality of relocation should be credited to the children who lost their lives in the fire, and to those who lost their lives in suicides. Now some Innu leaders want very much to take the credit, but I believe it was a team effort and the elders with their wisdom should also take credit. As for me, I once heard a man say in the news: it doesn't matter who takes the credit, as long as the job is done. And I know it was those children who turned the world's eyes towards us.

Innu protest camp at Emish (Voisey's Bay), 1995

HEALING

In the early 1990s, when the healing really began, we had a sober and energetic leader. He wanted to do something for all the sickness we had in our communities; he wanted to promote sobriety within the leadership of the Innu. At first I considered him the enemy. I always said nobody should tell us what to do, especially people from Sheshatshiu who always walk all over us and think they are always right. The decisions were always made by the people in Sheshatshiu, without the people in Davis Inlet having our say. For me it was all internal politics at first. Then I came to my senses. I knew we had to fight alcoholism; it was killing our people.

At the beginning of 1990, I tried to quit drinking on my own. I fell off the wagon many times. My first attempt to stay sober lasted six months. I was traveling all the time and I couldn't stop myself. In the midst of all my troubles and public pressures, I fell off the wagon again and again.

The meetings with the federal and provincial governments went on and on, taking my time and energy. Dealing with my own alcoholism was not my first priority. I couldn't care less about my family and myself. During the community gathering in April 1991, I fell off the wagon. I didn't care much about what was happening. I believed it would be the same routine. People would complain about the lousy job we did on the council, although the purpose of the meeting was to choose a new site for the community. We had fought hard to have our say.

The Premier had suggested a site with some services in place so that the governments wouldn't have to spend so much. He recommended that we look at three or more choices. One of them was Goose Bay. I was sure people in Goose Bay would oppose this; I later learned they'd had a meeting to find out what was going on. When the referendum was held in Davis Inlet, the majority voted for Natuashish, while the other site got only one percent of the vote. Only three people wanted to move to Goose Bay.

Through it all, I kept drinking. One night, I started fighting again with my wife. At the time she was carrying our fourth child. I woke up beside her and saw that her nose was filled with dried blood, and I woke her up to see if she was okay. She told me that she was leaving me. After promising her many times before that I would never hurt her, I didn't know what to do.

The next morning my mother came back to the tent, which she had left the evening before because of our drinking. She came back and started yelling at me; she said she could hear my wife screaming and yelling all through the night. Then my uncle came inside our tent to see what was happening. He, too, raised his voice to me. He said what I did was inexcusable. I had nobody to blame but myself if I seriously hurt my wife and the baby. He reminded me of how my first common-law wife died, something I had tried not to think about. He said I still didn't care how many people I hurt and now I was doing the same thing to my second wife.

When I was a teenager, the only way to become a man was to drink and have a wife. So when I was 17 I was making my own home brew and living with a common-law wife even younger than me. We ignored the disapproval of both our parents. I couldn't care less about what I did; I was just following the pack. The first few months were okay. I was acting civilized and felt I had a new lease on life. But after a few months, we grew tired of each other. The hurting, lying and cheating grew worse every day. I was constantly going on trips to outside meetings, as I was working for the NMIA (Naskapi Montagnais Innu Association, which later became the Innu Nation).

Other things changed as well. The slap I had given her on the wrist became a more aggressively clenched fist into her face. As my consumption of alcohol increased, my temper flared like a raging bull. I couldn't control the anger. I inflicted harm on her and I was in no position to seek help, even though I felt remorse and pain for what I did to her. I just couldn't control it. I must have apologized a million times and claimed that I would never do it again, but this only lasted a few days a month, when I was sober. I didn't do the things when I didn't drink. I wasn't in trouble with the law when I wasn't drinking.

Then something happened that will haunt me the rest of my life. I was in Goose Bay for meetings. My girlfriend and I had a good telephone conversation and she sounded happy. She said she was looking forward to me coming home. She asked me to bring her some clothes. After drinking the night before, I felt a bit hungover as we headed home on a charter plane on Good Friday. We landed on the harbour ice, and my drinking buddy picked me up. I hopped on his skidoo with a case of booze to keep my supporters happy.

As we arrived at my parents' house, I heard a commotion going on inside. As I went in, I saw my sister and brother holding my girlfriend in their arms. She had shot herself with a 22 rifle and was bleeding from her shoulder. I could see she was struggling to stand. I got her on my buddy's snowmobile and rushed her to the clinic. I screamed at the nurses to come and help me get her inside. We carried her to the bed and the nurses did the best they could. As she lay on the bed, she whispered to me that she was scared and worried. I told her not to worry; everything would be all right. I had once seen someone who had shot himself in the same area, and he was all right. I was certain she would be okay. But I sensed something wasn't right when I saw the blank faces of the nurses as one of them approached me. I was leaning towards my girlfriend and trying to speak to her. One of the nurses started sobbing and then I realized that I had lost her.

I thought I was sleeping and having a nightmare and I couldn't wake up. I went back to my parents and the whole clans were there, and I just couldn't say anything when two of my children were immediately taken away from me. One of them was a few months old and the other was two years old. In the next few months, I couldn't handle my grief and sorrow. I felt I was being deserted by my own people and treated as an outcast. I felt my life was worthless. A lot of people believed that I killed her,

People greeting the plane on the ice, 1970s

that I was the one who pulled the trigger. Walking on the road, I could hear whispers and giggles.

When I went to visit friends, some of their fathers warned their daughters to stay away from me because they would end up dead.

My parents also had to listen to the remarks of my girlfriend's parents. My father often told me to snap out of it, to face it and try to live a normal life. My mother told me to imagine what my girlfriend's parents must feel about losing a daughter. She told me that when she herself lost her first husband, she experienced the same situation. She said people were harsh and they only believed what they wanted to believe. Healing would take time and I could not ignore that. I had to face it and try to deal with it any way I could. I had frequent nightmares and I would wake in the middle of the night sweating and calling her name. This only led me to more drinking.

That spring I joined my parents as they traveled to Natuashish for the spring hunt. I stayed with them for a few months. During our stay, my father told me a story about a man who abused his wife. He said a man and wife stayed alone in the country with no children. The wife was a fine wife; she could sew moccasins perfectly and mend her husband's things. The man was a good hunter; he provided food for his wife. But the man would hit her with a stick and hurt her every chance he got. One night the man's wife died and from that moment on, the man felt pain and suffering. Every time he went out in his torn moccasins, he sang a song. "If only I hadn't abused my manhood. And now I feel the pain in every footstep as I go across the swamp and lakes." That day I swore that if I ever had another wife, I would not abuse her.

Years after my first wife died, I saw a mirror image of my young self in our first-born son. My son and his common-law wife stayed next door in an apartment for a few weeks when we were living in Goose Bay. I witnessed the anger and abuse he inflicted on his girlfriend. I immediately called the police to have him charged with assault. After he was taken away, I called Social Services to get help for his girlfriend. I offered her a one-way ticket out to stay with her relatives in Quebec.

But she refused and she was angry with me for reporting my son to the police. He asked for my help when he was in court and his lawyer came to me a number of times. I refused to support him. I later learned that the healing agencies of the band council drafted a letter of support on his behalf. The hardest thing I had to do was to write the judge saying that I was more concerned for his girlfriend and he had to think about what he had done. Today he struggles very hard to follow the right path. The only way for him to stay out of trouble is to lay off the alcohol.

My uncle gave me an earful the day after I hurt my second wife. I will never forget the words and sometimes when I think of him, his thundering voice aches my eardrums. I feel I owe him something. I treated him badly when he was still around, and I never had a chance to say I am sorry and to tell him I respected him. I still have the snowshoes he made for me.

> If I had listened to and respected elders like my uncle, I would have been a different man growing up in this sometimes hostile world of ours. I have heard many things about Davis Inlet in healing sessions — that evil spirits lie beneath the houses, that we built houses on ancient burial grounds and so brought misery and despair to the community. But I once heard somebody say in a healing session: "Hell is what we create ourselves. The misery, pain and suffering is what alcohol contributes." If we see the problem this way, we can work on it.

~Adeline Benuen, protestor at Innu camp, Emish, 1995.

Is Respect and Fairness for Aboriginal People too high a PRICE for VINCO?

WAKING THE TRUE INNU SPIRIT

What we needed next was an awakening. We had to resurrect the true Innu spirit to struggle with governments, protest changes to our land and heal our sickening souls. For me, the awakening came when I saw Innu protest against the military activity in Nitassinan. I saw the people of Sheshatshiu protesting while the police carried them away to waiting buses. I knew then that it was time to take new kinds of action to fight the ignorance of governments.

When we defied government policies, we created among ourselves intense feelings of empowerment. The military and law enforcement agencies had us in their grip for many years. Now we were finally breaking free. We could speak out and show the outside world what the Canadian government was doing in their own backyard to Aboriginal people. Since then, there has been a lot of support from other countries. Governments have changed their attitudes towards the Innu in Nitassinan. Once again, we can feel proud to be Innu. I can see it on the faces of the Innu in our communities.

> We had to look at how we got where we were. The young leaders had parents who abused alcohol. We followed the footsteps of our parents and other supposed role models. We followed the lead of the ones we hung out with when we were young, those who went to St. John's to finish high school.

When they came back to Davis Inlet, they dressed differently and wore their hair long. They seemed to understand a language we could not comprehend. They brought the rock and roll era home. Their rebellion against their elders and outside workers caught our attention, for we needed a new image to feed our bored adolescent minds. My peers and I grew out of our dreams of becoming great hunters and providers. Our new dreams were more European. We wanted to be teachers, store managers, hydro plant workers, the new positions created by the government.

When we saw our role models gain respect from the elders and the community, we wanted to be like them. We were very impressed with their English. They were always going out of Davis Inlet for meetings with the government. I wanted a job like that. Now, I think I was only looking at the alcohol they brought back and I wanted to do the same.

~Me and my daughter Linda

CROSSING THE WHITE LINE

In 1995 I moved with my family to Goose Bay. I had decided to enroll in ABE to try to finish my education. In Goose Bay, I could no longer do the things I loved—no more fishing and hunting and traveling on the land.

In the more urban setting of Goose Bay, there were cultural differences and lots of expenses.

With a family of seven (and maybe I can count myself as two persons because of my size), it was very hard to keep food on the table. There were car loans and insurance for the car. Everything the children did I had to pay for—minor hockey, soccer, games, swimming. They all required money that I didn't have because I was on a fixed income. Going back to school at the age of 33 brought a lot of gray hairs. It was hard to live up to family responsibilities with the sudden difference in income. For 17 years, I'd worked for the band council and Innu Nation. I was used to making a decent living.

> The second hard part of the transition was crossing the line to living in a White society. Perceptions of the Innu were different here. My children faced racism in school; they brought home new racist names they wondered about. It was something I was familiar with from my years of traveling back and forth to Goose Bay. Each time I encountered racism, it sent shock waves to my spine. Racism towards the Innu is as bad as anything you might hear

in the media in the United States. If nothing is done to fight racism in Goose Bay, things will only get worse, and the situation will go from name-calling to more destructive acts.

The first year was the hardest for my family. We met up with the racist idea that anybody with black hair has lice and is a carrier of diseases. My two boys were playing soccer and at the end of the game the players were lined up to shake hands and at least five children wouldn't even touch them.

Sometimes, their report cards had comments from the teachers that they lacked oral and written English skills. Some of those teachers realized that our first language is Innu-aimun and we used it a home all the time.

I would often hear that Aboriginal people had everything free—free education, free housing, no taxes. If the people who say this could see the houses we lived in, they would be ashamed. When CBC showed the deplorable housing conditions in northern Labrador in the late 1980s, the Canadian public was ashamed. The same conditions still existed. Shortages meant that sometimes 10 to 15 people shared

Nutshimit

a two or three-bedroom house. This was not acceptable by Canadian standards, but for the Innu it had always been the same. Every year government officials questioned our request for housing repairs. Why do you have to repair houses every year? Why don't you learn to keep your homes from breaking apart?

White society often forgets that the Innu are different. We used to live in tents or teepees made of caribou hides; these are our homes and we know how to build and repair them expertly. Like Whites, we know how to take care of the kind of dwellings we have traditionally lived in.

Free education is another scam. I have yet to see an educated Innu with a university degree working in Davis Inlet. Formal education was not a priority for the Innu, but that may be changing. When I went to do upgrading, a lot of people in the community followed my path. Then the Band Council set up a program for adult learners in partnership with the college in Goose Bay.

My experiences in Goose Bay changed my attitudes towards White people. I'd always thought people in Goose Bay were all racists, but I was wrong. There are a lot of good people who will remain my friends. I still see and talk to my classmates at the college and the others at the entrepreneurial courses I took. They had to get past racist attitudes towards the Innu, and they tried.

My own thinking changed in other ways too. I had believed that all Innu should live in country and live the traditional way of life. But now I had chosen to live in this White, urban culture. I wanted my children to be ready to face whatever challenges came along. I wanted this to be one of the experiences that would prepare them to face the difficulties that I struggled with when I was growing up. I knew that, like me, they would be caught between worlds.

Now I was also caught between responsibilities. When I decided to enroll in ABE, I felt I was deserting my duties as a community leader, neglecting the needs of the people, leaving the files I had been working on unresolved. The decision I faced kept me awake at night; questions kept pounding me. What sort of person am I? Why am I doing this? What do I have to gain in doing this? The questions would not let me rest the first few months in Goose Bay. Am I running away from my friends? Do they feel deserted by me?

We, the young leaders, took on a lot because we had few resources from the outside. We had to do everything ourselves, and we were expected to do a lot. Nothing we did could be enough to solve Davis Inlet's problems. We were under a lot of pressure.

Sometimes I blamed myself for contributing to the social illness that haunts Davis Inlet. Sometimes I wondered whether we were making the right decisions for our own people.

I needed a change, a break from all the sudden changes we lived with in the community. I needed a new way of thinking. And I knew that the problems and the negotiations with governments—all that struggle—would still be there whenever I returned.

I am constantly in struggle with my inner soul to overcome the barriers that I am about to face. I know that education will be rewarding and will help me in my work. I want to write fluently. But I always question the path I am taking. I tell myself I can always go back. But will I?

~ My ancestors, including Sam and Raphael Rich

WHERE I BELONG

My parents raised me to be free. I could stay with other family members like my sisters or brothers for a period of time. Every time my parents wanted me to stay in the country or stay in the bay for the fall, I hid and avoided them so I could stay in Davis Inlet with my sister or brother. I was used to the new community by now. I especially liked the movies the priest showed on Thursdays and Sundays. My parents always seemed to know where I was staying.

I have good and bad memories of growing up in Davis Inlet. I remember looking forward to Halloween and Christmas. Near Christmas, the Hercules military jets would fly around the community to parachute Christmas supplies for the missionary to hand out. It was fascinating to watch the supplies getting thrown out of those big planes and the parachutes coming down slowly from the sky. The only other time we ever saw parachutes was in war movies. The crates would sometimes hit hard on recently frozen ice and all the goodies inside would be all over the place. As children, we would run towards them, ignoring the priest yelling that we should be careful or we'd get hit by crates. The high winds sometimes carried the parachuted crates into a wooded area. It was an opportunity for young men to search and hide some of the stuff they claimed they found.

I also have fond memories of Natuashish, where I partly grew up and where my parents camped in the spring and fall. As soon as there was open water in early spring, my father would set his net for Arctic char as they headed back to the salt

My father Napaien with speared Arctic char

water. The spring would bring warm weather and we would wake to the sounds of sparrows and the crackling of sparks in my mother's fire. She would be cooking the fresh Arctic char that my father caught. Natuashish, about seven kilometres north of Davis Inlet, is surrounded by rolling hills covered with evergreens. I recall the quiet and beauty of the pond with the morning mist rising from the cold water, and the lonely cries of the great northern diver. I believe that people in Davis Inlet have made the right choice when they decided to spend the rest of their lives in Natuashish.

My parents usually adopted a couple of teenage boys to tag along with us to Natuashish, and the parents of those young men didn't mind at all. Nowadays, if I wanted to take somebody with me, there would be the red tape of Social Services. My background would be checked; they would want to know whether I use alcohol or drugs. We forget that it takes a whole community to raise a child. Long ago, the people of Davis Inlet lived with this 'new' motto that I often hear now at healing conferences.

My friends and I once went on a hike to the other side of our island. We climbed a hill and went down the other side, farther than we'd planned. We played hide and seek, running around in a wooded area. Eventually, we ended up on the other end of the island. We were sitting and lying down on the shore when we heard an outboard motor. We were about six miles away from Davis Inlet. The sun was slowly setting and it would have been dark before we made it home. After hiking through the swamps, tired and hungry, we lay on a flat rock and talked about what we wanted to do when we grew up. One of my friends said he would marry and make love to his wife all the time and have a lot of children. Others said they wanted to have a skidoo or a fast speedboat.

We lay listening to the outboard motor approaching. I suppose the people on the boat saw us with their binoculars. They headed in our direction and landed their punts on the sandy area of the beach. It was my uncle Kaniuekutat after hauling his catch. He wasn't surprised to see us. He called us crazy kids and asked if our mothers knew where we were. He told us to go home directly as he had little room in his boat, and there were at least five of us. As he was ready to start his outboard motor, he grunted to us to go with him. I felt relieved and was glad to be in the boat. I had dreaded going back to Davis Inlet overland in the dark of the night. It was slightly dark when we made it back.

I was sure that this would not be the last I'd hear from my uncle. The next morning he visited and told my mother where he'd found us. He said she should know better than to let her 12-year-old son wander miles away from home. My mother was a wise woman; she never said anything as she had always shown respect and admiration to her older brother. My mother was never the type of person who would yell at us.

Until I was 15, my parents protected me from harm and disciplined me away from any wrongdoing. Our parents told us all—five boys and one girl—that we should never make fun of our elders and try to help out where we can. My mother said that, because elders had certain gifts from our creators, if we supported them we would probably live just as long as they did. When I reached the age of 17, I soon forgot this. But I remember it now.

> On any paths we follow in our lives there are always hurdles and curves before one can reach one's destination. Sometimes the paths that we follow can lead to the destruction of a life; any wrong turn can lead this way.
>
> Gradually we can reach the place we want to go, but the tricky part is we can only identify it when we get there.

I decided to follow the path of well-being and it has led me to sobriety ever since 1991. I remember what my late uncle Kaniuekutat said to me. He said, "It's not going to be easy," and it's not easy. It's not easy to let out all my anger and what is eating me away inside, to reveal my inner soul and welcome the combined strength of family and friends. But I wouldn't be here today if I was still sucking on that bottle of destruction. I am much happier now than I ever was. I have a wonderful wife and five children. I have the rest of my life.

My family with wife Penash and our children, from left to right back row, Mathias, Ken David, Gilbert, Rachel, and adopted son Sam

Our old family home in Utshimassits

EPILOGUE

THE ROCKY ROAD TO SELF-DETERMINATION

"Aww, are you sure? It can't be!" Penash said. "It should be ready by now. A lot of people are out there, and I've already packed everything up."

My wife sounded very disappointed and frustrated when I told her that our house was not ready for us to move in. I had driven to check on it earlier that morning. The frozen ice was smooth, making my trip faster. As I drove off the skidoo trail on to the snow-plowed road, I encountered trucks and tractor trailers, making last minute deliveries of furniture or doing final inspections on the homes. Apart from these vehicles, the streets were empty. Not a soul was walking this early morning as I arrived in the new community of Natuashish. I couldn't see any skidoo traffic because few people had moved here yet, or maybe they were enjoying the warm comforts of their new home.

"Trucks, fuel trucks even. Oh my!" I said to myself. I was witnessing the first big change to our lives in this new community. We would now have roads, trucks, snow plows, a telephone technician vehicle.

I could not visit anyone because I didn't know where my relatives lived. I toured the town, driving over the cleared road, and finally reached our new house. I entered to see if anyone was there. I witnessed a few carpenters at work. "It'll be ready within the week for you to move in," they told me. They still needed to put another coat of paint on the walls, and to place the tiles on the floor. The house cleaners also would be in to straighten everything out.

"Check in with the site office. Call them and they'll know when your house is ready," they told me.

I guessed it wouldn't hurt to wait another week.

I couldn't believe that we had actually done it. We had managed to get new homes with running water. My house had four bedrooms and a washroom with a bath and shower. This would be quite a change for my family, as in Davis Inlet we only had a two-bedroom house. We had just adopted our baby boy Sam, and now our children would each have their own room.

I felt such happiness and a lot of hope for the future.

As I drove back to Davis Inlet, I must have shed a few tears. There were three different ways to get back to the village, the seaside way, through the centre of the island and a wooded area, or along the south side of the island, which was the way I decided to go that morning. I was thinking about the children, how they would have a chance, new opportunities. I was thinking about how the people would have to change somehow for the better. I drove across Daniel's Rattle and on to Davis Inlet, along the clearly-marked skidoo trail. I encountered a few skidoos as they journeyed to see their new houses.

I know how my family is feeling, I thought to myself. This is actually happening.

It wasn't long before the phones were working in the new community, and we were able to keep in touch with the workers. My family waited patiently for a few days. We were told the house would be completed by Christmas. Just imagine the excitement—our first Christmas in our new home, our new community. This was something we would never forget.

Finally we moved in. I can still see the excitement in my children's eyes as they threw off their snowsuits and winter boots. Their faces were shining with anticipation for better things to come. Despite the cold trip traveling from Davis Inlet to the new site, their mouths were wide with huge grins as they stepped in to explore this large new house. The very first thing they did was claim their bedrooms.

This would be the place where my children would have their own families. Hopefully they would not encounter the pain and misery we had seen growing up on the small island of Davis Inlet. This was a place of hope, a place where our spirits were connected to the mainland, where our ancestors had camped and fished for thousands of years. We could feel a connection with these ancestors as we entered our new homes in this new community of Natuashish. My wife and I joined our children in their excitement. We also felt the presence of the people we had lost in Davis Inlet. They would never see this relocation, but their spirits remained in our hearts, and we knew they would continue to look upon us from the heavens above. They too were sharing in this moment as we entered another chapter in our lives, this new beginning for the next generation.

We now had a wood and oil furnace and we would just need to make a call to have oil delivered right to our homes. This was a change from Davis Inlet, where the pump was always broken and it was such a hassle to fill up the tank.

My children wanted to take a shower and clean up right away. It was such a feeling of joy and accomplishment. We had fought for many years so that our children could have running water and a good home.

Meanwhile the Innu leadership was concerned that without programs and services to help us tackle the problems we faced back in Davis Inlet, we could expect to face the same issues in Natuashish. After the move we soon began to see social problems and media headlines. The National Post headline read "Former Davis Inlet community's problems persist despite new start."

The Globe and Mail reported "A decade after the people of Davis Inlet were relocated, they are still hunting demons."

We held numerous meetings with both levels of government to continue to push for the Innu agenda.

"Give us the tools and resources we need so we can do this ourselves," we told them.

> But our voices fell on deaf ears all over again. We insisted to the people who were criticizing the move, including the Newfoundland public, that if new houses and a move to a new community were the remedy to all our social ills, Canada would surely be such a healthy place to live. We argued that if we had other illnesses such as diabetes, heart disease or even cancer, we would still have those ailments in a new community. They were not going away.

Former Chief Simeon Tshakapesh explained this eloquently in a CBC interview.

"Giving homes, heat and running water helps, but solving the community's problems will take time," he said. "Problems don't go away by moving into a new house. It will take time."

And with time, this is what we have done. The Innu of Natuashish have worked with great effort to heal the community. We passed a by-law banning alcohol and drugs in 2007, and the ban worked for years. The problems associated with substance abuse greatly diminished. Then drug dealers and bootleggers came out of the woodwork. The police were authorized to enforce the ban and they seized hundreds of bottles of alcohol and a lot of illegal drugs. It was a sad thing to witness our own people cash in on people's misery. Soon we saw people who had no work, nor income, driving new trucks and new snowmobiles, buying new toys for their children. We began to see the problems created by banning alcohol and drugs.

We were lucky to find some people outside in freezing conditions before it was too late. But one person died of exposure when his skidoo broke down not far from

Davis Inlet. The two people traveling on the skidoo were headed to Natuashish on their way back from Hopedale on a booze run. After the skidoo refused to start again, they kept walking through blinding snow. Luckily the second person survived, although he also came close to dying of exposure.

The problem is a complex one to deal with. There are ways to tackle drug dealers and bootleggers—to get people to stop drinking or taking drugs altogether. We still need outside support and expertise to deal with these problems. At one point in Davis Inlet, we had an 80 percent level of sobriety because of the support we received from Health Canada. They sent an outside person to support us. The rest was up to us and today there are still a lot of people in Natuashish who have maintained their sobriety. I have always believed that our community needs professionals to deal with our alcohol and drug problems, to resolve our social ills, but we still do not have this support today.

A lot of people live a sober life in Natuashish. There are struggles, but I have seen people making choices for a healthy lifestyle. We will always have problems, like any other community in Canada. People say time heals, and that is what I see happening.

> There are more good things happening in Natuashish than ever before. We have a much higher number of high school graduates. That is one of our success stories since we took over control of our schools. Setting up our own school board was a major task and accomplishment. It could still be a tremendous success if we had active board members more able to implement new ideas and deal with school issues. Unfortunately that is not happening at the moment.

We still don't have adequately trained Innu teachers or a strong Innu language program in the classroom. We need these to preserve our language and culture. We see the dangers of losing our language because our grandchildren are speaking more and more English. The sad part is that young parents speak to their kids in English, and even more sadly the grandparents are doing the same thing. If we force ourselves to speak to our children and grandchildren in our mother tongue,

the language will live on for a long time. A strong and active promotion of Innu-aimun in our schools could involve the implementation of an Innu-aimun immersion program in the early grades. I've often heard people say that without our language, our cultural identity will be lost forever.

We are still working on taking over our child welfare programs. The Innu leadership has a constant battle on their hands with this issue. Numerous Innu children are involved in the province's Child Youth and Family Services (CFYS) system. These children have been taken away from their parents and placed in foster homes outside our communities. The government's social workers say the children are not safe, that they are facing violence in their homes, and that their homes are overcrowded. The province spends millions of dollars housing our children outside of Natuashish and Sheshatshiu, and it pays a good dollar to the people who look after them.

We keep insisting to both the provincial and federal governments that they should spend this money to house the children in our communities, so that they won't lose their language and culture. Governments should also invest in support services parents need, like parenting programs or a family treatment program. Governments have also told us they can't fund an education program to train Innu high school graduates to be social workers, yet they continue to spend so much on band-aid solutions.

Governments need to think outside the box. As usual, they deny our requests, stating that we do not have rights over our own children. We have been dealing with the ignorance of governments most of our lives. Our children are taken away to other parts of Canada and the province, and they often come back urban children. They act and dress differently. They don't fit in. There is a total disregard of the Innu culture when it comes to foster parents. Our children come back speaking only the English language. Some of these children have committed suicide.

Finally after many years of lobbying, the federal government has agreed to fund a group home to shelter children in Natuashish so that they are not taken away.

⟵ Toon, myself and Kiti, with Shushep, my mother Matnin and Etet

However, this is a minor solution to a much larger problem. As of March 2017, we have at least 196 children 'in need of protection' according to CYFS. There are foster parents available here in Natuashish and I am sure there are some in Sheshatshiu. We have homes to take in these children. The ongoing attitude of the province on this matter translates into a policy of destroying the language and culture of Innu children.

My wife and I have fostered children for many years now. CYFS placed a baby in our home and we have legally adopted him. We still have two more foster children living with us now. These two do not come from a violent home. We can't figure out why they were removed from their own home in the first place.

The community still has a long way to go but we will get there. As my late Aunt Utshimaskueu always used to say, "the cleaning of the caribou hide takes time, but little by little it will change for the better."

There are other major changes happening in our communities. These involve hard decisions that need to be made. One of these has to do with land claims, a process that has been going on for at least 30 years. According to the Innu Nation website, we first tabled a land claim in 1977. Both levels of government turned it down. They said we did not have sufficient evidence that we occupied the lands we were claiming. Back then the Innu Nation was known as the Naskapi Montagnais Innu Association. The federal government was saying they wanted the Innu to prove that they were the original owners of Labrador. They were asking us to do a historic and current land use and occupancy study to determine that we indeed had used and continued to use this land.

I first heard the word land claims back in 1974 when our Naskapi cousins from Kawawachikamach came to Davis Inlet for a meeting to discuss land claims with our elders at the time. They talked to the people about issues in Quebec relating to land rights negotiations. I was still a young lad back then, with a lack of knowledge of how other Innu from Quebec lived and survived. People heard later that the James Bay and Northern Quebec Agreement was signed, but nobody in Davis Inlet knew much about the land claims process. Even today people are still struggling with the concept of asking for the land that has been ours since time immemorial.

It was during the summer of 1991 when the communities of Davis Inlet and Sheshatshiu held a gathering to discuss various issues, including the military low-level flying, land claims, and how to deal with governments that continued to bypass us when dealing with developments on our lands. There was also a lot of talk about the possible damming of another of our rivers, and about the exploration companies who had claimed tens of thousands of mining stakes all over our lands without consulting the Innu leadership. We spoke to elders about beginning talks with the governments on land rights, to see how far we could go. The meeting lasted for a few days, and a number of questions kept coming up. Should we oppose the mining companies or hydro developments on our lands? Should we continue to fight against the destruction of our land that has sustained our people for centuries? These questions lingered in the minds of the Innu leadership for months and years. We held meeting after meeting amongst ourselves about where we saw our people 20 or 30 years into the future.

During this time we also negotiated with companies to get impact benefit agreements (IBAs). The negotiation of these IBAs was a result of a community decision to address the fact that we did not have any funding to build our growing communities. These IBAs were also seen as the only way to get at least something out of our resources from our lands. It was a hard decision to make.

Today, we are still fighting both levels of governments for breadcrumbs. We need new houses, new infrastructure, education, new programs and services. We are still struggling to get extra funding for basic things we need in our communities.

We know the government policies in dealing with Aboriginal peoples. They will give us as little as they can until we have signed all our resources away. We are not masters at the governments' negotiating table. A lot of people in our communities

∼ Signing of the Tshash Petapan New Dawn Agreement,
Standing: Simon Poker, Sebastien Benuen, Ed Martin, John Olthuis, Joseph Rich, Kathy Dunderdale, Akat Piwas, Peter Penashue, Monique Rich, Mary jane Nui, Dominic Pokue, Sam Nui, George Rich, Mark Nui.
Seated: Sebastien Penunsi, Ponus Nuke, Ann Philomena Pokue, Etuet Piwas, Shimun Michael, Jaochim Nui, Elizabeth Rich.

lack education, but we have a lot of experience observing governmental ignorance and lack of respect for our people and our lands. There are a few people within the Innu leadership who are fluent in English and understand the ways of the governments. We have learned things the hard way, and we continue to speak out on behalf of other Innu people who can't speak for themselves. Over the years, elders have been invited to attend land rights meetings, and a lot of them have spoken at those meetings, sharing their experience and knowledge about the animals they hunted and the land they knew growing up.

Although we hardly have any experience in dealing with the entity that has successfully been dominating indigenous peoples for 500 years, we know about all the broken promises and twisted words that make it sound as if governments actually care for Aboriginal peoples. Although we have never surrendered our Indigenous rights, nor sold our lands, Canada's agenda is very clear—we must concede our rights and forgive them of past wrongdoings. Governments and their agents always have the upper hand at the table, where we sit opposite whole departments. They have the last say. Their regulations and policies have continuously downgraded and dismissed our exhausting input on the issues we want to discuss. Our land rights negotiators echo this view about the difficulties at the negotiating table—the government approach is wrong.

We know we will be forced to surrender our land and extinguish our rights for all that is sacred to our heart and soul, along with the rights of our future grandchildren, generations that have yet to enjoy our lands, the animals, the trees, and waters.

We know other treaties and land claims agreements in Canada have complied with Canada's demand to extinguish Indigenous rights and title to the land.

Governments have many resources at the table. Federal and provincial negotiators keep changing every few years, so new ones have to be educated. When these negotiators don't agree with what's already been settled, they use delay tactics. Each new negotiator reads every chapter carefully. Innu negotiators just keep pushing the issues that are important to us, including how Innu should have the right to hunt on the land without permits, and the inclusion of future IBA requirements within economic development zones.

Although many of our people have never seen our land rights negotiators in action, these negotiators fight hard for the people. I have seen people continue to criticize the main table negotiators at the Innu Nation AGM (annual general meeting), but what they fail to realize is that every comment or suggestion they make to the Innu Nation leadership and its negotiators, has already been mentioned at the negotiating table.

Innu leaders know it is hard to get the Innu agenda across to experienced government officials. The results are not always great. It is hard to trust governments, which is why we have lawyers who understand the concepts of negotiations. I have had the opportunity to witness first hand the negotiations for impact benefits agreements and land rights, and I have seen our lawyers fight very hard. Emotions sometimes run extremely high. I have seen frustration and anger at the table. We have fought hard to get those agreements. We also fought mining and hydroelectric companies to ensure that we received financial benefits, including access to training and jobs.

People should know that you don't always get what you want at the negotiating table.

Indigenous peoples must go through this process if they want to settle a land claims. We signed a land claims framework agreement in 1996, which identified the issues we would discuss. In 2011 Innu Nation leaders signed an agreement-in-principle. I was at the signing ceremony. This formed the basis for the Tshash Petapan New Dawn Agreement, which actually includes three agreements: 1) the Lower Churchill Impact Benefit Agreement, 2) the Churchill Falls Hydro Redress Agreement, and 3) the Innu Rights Agreement in principal. This package of agreements first had to be ratified by the people of the two communities. We put it to a vote and 70 % of our eligible voters turned out. Of those voters, 88% voted to support the package. The vote was held after the Innu Nation held community consultation meetings in both Natuashish and Sheshatshiu, during which it was explained to those who attended what was contained in the agreements.

This is how I see it. Innu critics of the agreements have stated that the Innu Nation bought this vote by bribing the people with a $5,000 payout. This was not the case at all. The payouts were in response to people from the two communities asking their leadership for a payout to buy items they needed for their homes, among other things. Even today people are still asking for these payouts. Sometimes the Innu leadership gives in because the money all comes from a trust fund set up with resources from IBAs—from Innu land resources. This practice follows our Innu tradition of sharing. It is the same concept followed when people go caribou hunting. When there is meat to share, the *utshimau* or leader of the hunt, shares it. The two Band Councils have to look after their communities first.

The government continues to give us loans to enable us to be at the negotiation table with them. As we near 25 years in official negotiations, the debt from these loans has grown to a significant amount. Even if we settle land claims today, we will have nothing left over at the end of the day, when the debt is called in. It is a time-consuming business dealing with the governments.

> It is now March 2017. The final agreement on land claims is just around the corner and community consultations are taking place to prepare people for another vote. Regardless of the decisions we make as a community, good or bad, these agreements once signed will always be in the public domain. It will remain to be seen by future generations if we did the right thing or not on their behalf. History will be the judge.

Ongoing community consultations are being held to try to educate the Natuashish and Sheshatshiu Innu about what we will be putting to a vote. There seem to be a lot of people feeling alienated in the face of this complex land rights agreement. It is hard to comprehend and difficult to discuss within our communities. We have to create new words in Innu-aimun. The legal language is the most difficult to understand. Innu interpreters sometimes use English words when they are translating for the Innu public, making it hard for elders and those who don't have any education to understand what they need to know before the final vote. People have to ask questions, and if they are not satisfied with the answers they receive, they have to keep asking questions, until they are fully satisfied with the response.

The agreement document is inches thick. It includes maps that show different categories of land: the Labrador Innu Settlement Area and the Labrador Innu Lands. On these lands we have different types of rights or control over hunting and fishing, over who gets to build a cabin and where, who gets to explore for minerals or petroleum, and who gets to go ahead with resource development. The need for companies to negotiate IBAs with the Innu, and how revenues from resource developments will be shared with the Innu, are also outlined. The agreement states that we can pass these rights on to our children.

There are pages in the agreement about conservation, and the management and harvesting of wildlife, migratory birds, fish, forest and plant resources. The agreement defines how the Innu will not have the right to sell wildlife we harvest, but we can give or trade with other Innu or Aboriginal people. There is a section on water rights, another on the Akami-uapishk^u-KakKasuak-Mealy Mountains National Park, and another on archaeological resources.

The agreement also spells out when and how we will have to share some of these powers with governments or other Aboriginal peoples. I don't like the section on expropriation—the power of Canada or the province to buy Innu land to use for purposes set out under their laws. But the agreement does limit how much land governments could expropriate. It also requires governments to consult with the Innu before expropriation and to provide the Innu with alternative lands for those being expropriated. Finally the agreement spells out what rights the Innu will continue to have in the Voisey's Bay and Mishta-shipu areas.

One of the consultation meetings the land rights team held was with Natuashish students from grades 8 to level 3. We are trying to encourage our young people to complete their education, because they will be the ones who will take over this agreement once the Innu of Natuashish and Sheshatshiu ratify it. Our youth will have to step up and be the leaders. We told the students we are going to need environmentalists to look after the lands and waters, and biologists to look after the marine and wildlife. We will need business people with degrees in commerce, accountants to look after our finances, people who will ensure we are spending our dollars in a way that will continue to benefit future generations.

Most importantly, the hope is that the Innu will be able to enjoy their way of life, that they will maintain a balance and continue practicing our culture on the lands that have sustained us for thousands of years. We will be in control and we will have the final say about who is going to develop mines and other resources. This is what I understand from reading this agreement and being part of the land rights team. But every person in our community must see and learn about this agreement for him or herself.

The land rights negotiation team will first present the contents of the deal to the Innu Nation leadership—both the good and the bad, the benefits and the compromises. The team will then present it to the people for their approval. It is really up to the people of Natuashish and Sheshatshiu if they want to see this deal finalized. Our collective future is in all of our hands. Each of us in our minds and with our votes will change the course of history for future generations. As we decide, we must all remember that our vote will not only affect the people, but also our beautiful land upon which we have lived for thousands of years.

THE ROCKY ROAD TO SELF-DETERMINATION

Sam Rich, Meshkeia, my paternal grandfather

ACKNOWLEDGEMENTS

This book was developed for Exploring Memory, Finding Meaning, a special project of the Adult Basic Education Writing Network. We offer our thanks to the National Literacy Secretariat for their financial support of the book series.

We are grateful to a number of photographers, whose images grace the pages of this book: Georg Henriksen (p. 3), Hans Hvide Bang, (11, 28, 38, 64), Gary and Joanie McGuffin (14, 18-9, 68-9 and the cover), Heng Lin (p. 22), Joel Rich (44, 52), Alex Andrew (58-9), Valérie Courtois (90), Ken Rich (76, 80-1), and Camille Fouillard (32, 56). A number of photographs taken in the 1970s are part of the Davis Inlet Roman Catholic Mission Collection. Permission for their use was granted by Father Jack Davis (p. 4-5, 9, 24, 25, 26, 34, 40-1, 48-9, 70). Other photos are part of the Hettasch Collection, taken by Siegfried and Kate Hettasch (17, 62 and cover). Copies and permission for their use were provided by Hannie Fitzgerald. We also received permission from a number of institutions for the use of images in their collections: the Peary-MacMillan Arctic Museum and Arctic Studies Center (88); the National Museum of the American Indian, Smithsonian Institution (catalogue #: 17/6575) (ii); and the National Museums of Canada, Canadian Museum of Civilization (III-B-588) (36). Our thanks also to Helen Woodrow who provided digital versions of photographs included in the first edition of this book.

Every photograph has its own story and sometimes those stories were shared over late-night lunches. We thank everyone for trusting us with their slides, negatives and prints, and for the hot tea. Photograph searches also require some detective work. In our search, we depended on the extensive knowledge and assistance of Peter Armitage and Camille Fouillard. Camille also introduced us to George.

Participants and staff at the Rabbittown Learners Program in St. John's, the Learning Centre in Edmonton, and the Discovery Centre in Bay Roberts field tested earlier drafts of the books. Their comments and suggestions helped us improve the series.